Ladies Set Apart
for a Purpose

DEVON CHESTNUT

Ladies Set Apart for a Purpose

ISBN: 069236370X
ISBN-13: 978-0692363706

Cover page designed by Styles Print.

Unless otherwise indicated, all scripture quotations are taken from the New International Version (NIV) of the Bible.

Scripture quotations designated NIV are from THE HOLY BIBLE, NEW INTERNATIONAL VERSION®, NIV® Copyright © 1973, 1978, 1984, 2011 by Biblica, Inc.® Used by permission. All rights reserved worldwide.

DEDICATION

This book is to help young ladies like yourself understand that living the life God has planned for you can be amazing, fun, and is definitely worth living! People may say or do hurtful things to you but know that their negative actions do not determine who you are as a person. You are a lady set apart for a purpose!

Devon Chestnut

Ladies Set Apart for a Purpose

CONTENTS

ACKNOWLEDGMENTS

To my Heavenly Father for wisdom on completing this book. He gets all of the glory!

My spiritual parents Dr. Shannon & Pastor Shelia Cook for your leadership and teaching me how to tap into the wisdom of God.

Edwin Jr. & Yolanda Chestnut, my loving parents for your continual support.

Charmaine Neil, my beautiful grandmother inside and out.

Styles Print for the amazingly designed book cover.

Create Space for printing the book.

All of the youth that are such an inspiration.

All of you that purchased this book. Thank you!

FOREWORD

When we think of Devon Chestnut what comes to mind are two words. The first word is Purity. She is a person who has a pure heart that exudes the compassion and love of God. She is always driven to empower others to achieve this same pureness of heart. Devon not only teaches purity but she lives it on a daily basis.

The second word is Purpose. She is a person that understands her purpose and pursues it relentlessly. She is now on a mission to duplicate her success in the lives of millions around the world. The principles that she will share with you are guaranteed to catapult you into a place of purpose.

We are so proud to support and endorse this amazing book that is sure to impact lives in an uncommon way.

Dr. Shannon & Pastor Shelia Cook
Pastors, Dunamis World Outreach Church

CHAPTER 1

===

BEAUTIFUL IS HER NAME

TRUTH IS:

A lot of people put so much pressure on everyone nowadays comparing themselves, by wanting to look like or look better than someone else. Either they want a lighter or browner skin tone than the next, a bigger or smaller booty than the next, or being skinnier or thicker than another female to be more appealing. All of us women have the same parts but the size should not determine your beauty or who you are as a person. As a lady, do not put the next lady down because of how she looks. All of us are more than beautiful because we are created in the image and likeness of God. God is beyond beautiful!

TRUE STORY:

I'm a 5'10" slender female and a majority of the time I used to get criticized by women that had a thicker frame than me or women not as tall as me a lot. These women never knew there was a time I was not confident in who I was having a small frame, tall, easy to lose weight but hard to gain. All throughout school, I've heard so many negative and some positives names referring to my size and height. Even though at times the names were hurtful, I would not allow anyone to see that it hurt, defending myself and having comebacks. It took me years to even wear a pair of shorts.

After a while, I felt like if people could not appreciate me the way I am, so what! One day, I stood back and took a look at myself in the mirror and with my head lifted up high and shoulders pulled back I said to myself, "Devon, no matter what people say, you are beautiful just the way God made you"! No, I did not say this out of pride but I said it with confidence!

Now, you cannot stop me from wearing 4-6 inch stiletto heels and I do so boldly towering over others! Years later, I found out the same people that were making those mean remarks actually wanted what God gave me, the extra height. Regardless if you are short or tall, big or small, make the best of how you were made and love yourself! People are always going to have stuff to say but their words do not determine who you are as a person. Only the word of God and the words that come out of your mouth determine who you are always! After all, you have to live with yourself during this lifetime so be happy in your own skin.

CONFESSION:

I am beautiful the way God made me. I will carry myself as a lady at all times, with high standards and high expectations. I will not change anything about me because He does not create anything ugly. I don't care what people say about me, I am beautiful and only my words about myself matter.

INTRODUCTION

You do not have to experience mental or physical suffering from the words of people, on the way you look and the things that happened, in your past. Do not give excuses for not living up to the standards of others just because you do not think, act, or talk like them. Just do not compromise or give up! Compromising may seem like the thing that really makes you fit in with everyone else making everything seem right. You really know the truth though! That is why you feel uncomfortable when you keep trying to blend in with the crowd. It is a great thing you are different because you were set apart for a reason.

CHAPTER 1

BEAUTIFUL IS HER NAME

TRUTH IS:

A lot of people put so much pressure on everyone nowadays comparing themselves, by wanting to look like or look better than someone else. Either they want a lighter or browner skin tone than the next, a bigger or smaller booty than the next, or being skinnier or thicker than another female to be more appealing. All of us women have the same parts but the size should not determine your beauty or who you are as a person. As a lady, do not put the next lady down because of how she looks. All of us are more than beautiful because we are created in the image and likeness of God. God is beyond beautiful!

TRUE STORY:

I'm a 5'10" slender female and a majority of the time I used to get criticized by women that had a thicker frame than me or women not as tall as me a lot. These women never knew there was a time I was not confident in who I was having a small frame, tall, easy to lose weight but hard to gain. All throughout school, I've heard so many negative and some positives names referring to my size and height. Even though at times the names were hurtful, I would not allow anyone to see that it hurt, defending myself and having comebacks. It took me years to even wear a pair of shorts.

After a while, I felt like if people could not appreciate me the way I am, so what! One day, I stood back and took a look at myself in the mirror and with my head lifted up high and shoulders pulled back I said to myself, "Devon, no matter what people say, you are beautiful just the way God made you"! No, I did not say this out of pride but I said it with confidence!

Now, you cannot stop me from wearing 4-6 inch stiletto heels and I do so boldly towering over others! Years later, I found out the same people that were making those mean remarks actually wanted what God gave me, the extra height. Regardless if you are short or tall, big or small, make the best of how you were made and love yourself! People are always going to have stuff to say but their words do not determine who you are as a person. Only the word of God and the words that come out of your mouth determine who you are always! After all, you have to live with yourself during this lifetime so be happy in your own skin.

CONFESSION:

I am beautiful the way God made me. I will carry myself as a lady at all times, with high standards and high expectations. I will not change anything about me because He does not create anything ugly. I don't care what people say about me, I am beautiful and only my words about myself matter.

CHAPTER 2

=====================================

DON'T UNDERAPPRECIATE,
JUST APPRECIATE

DRUM ROLL:

So many times we appreciate so much what other people have and do not take the time out to appreciate the things that we have already. Just because it looks like they have more or it looks better than what you have, that does not mean that it is always better. You really do not want what someone else has if you know what they had to do to get there....... Do you?   Well, lets see.

REAL TALK:

Have you ever wanted something someone else had or has to the point where you wished you were them, making them an idol? That used to be me.

Several years after graduating college and still considered fresh to the working world, there was this one lady a little older than me that had everything a woman could possibly want! It seemed like she had it all together from the latest cars, stylish clothes, a couple of attractive men waiting on her hand and foot, and roses every day. Some of the ladies were like, "Dang! How did she do that"? After a while she no longer had happiness. She looked sad and like life was dragging her down. She received a wake up call about the guys, found out the truth, and everything was taken away from her. Everything from the cars down to the house was gone. I used to chat with her when I saw her and provided encouragement, from the word of God. She really appreciated it. I just prayed for her to find her joy in the Lord and not a man. Happiness is a temporary satisfaction, which you get from things like cars and money. Joy is everlasting and regardless of what things you have or do not have, keep or lose, nothing can make you sad. Now what if I would have done the same things, wishing I was like her?

I may not have lost it immediately but would have eventually lost everything because it was not a pleasing lifestyle to God. You have to be careful and not anxiously want what someone else has because 1) You do not know what they did to get it. 2) Will you be willing to do the same thing to get what they have? 3) Will it be worth it?

CONFESSION:

I will not make any person or thing an idol by trying to be like them, copying their every move, wishing I have everything they own. I cherish and value my life. I will be the best me I can be to get the things in life that were purposed only for me.

Psssttt... Can I let you in on a secret?

You are not missing out on anything

by living your own life.

STOP

wishing your life away.

CHAPTER 3

THAT MOUTH

LIFE AND YOUR MOUTH:

The heart cannot be seen but is a powerful organ. Think about it. Your heart gives life with every beat and once it stops, there is no more life. The tongue is another powerful body part because one word said about a person can do two things: 1) uplift them or 2) destroy them.

SHOULD I OR SHOUDN'T I:

Lied on talked about or were you the one doing the lying or talking about someone else? What is the reason for you doing it? Is it to try and hurt someone so they can feel the same pain you felt? Is it to ruin someone's reputation only to find out there was some jealousy behind it? Have you ever heard jealousy is a disease?

It is because it can get you to a point of wanting bad things happening to a person and you getting sick symptoms because of bitterness and the thought of revenge. You should walk in love at all times. If you truly do not have anything positive to say, keep that mouth of yours closed.

Now, we know not to pour cleaning bleach in someone's ear, right? Yes because it can damage the ear and other parts of the body to the point where it eats through, burns, and destroys it. That is the same way with spreading rumors and gossip, it is deadly. So think twice before talking bad about somebody whether you know the whole situation or not. What I am about to say may be the total opposite of what you want to do. If other people are spreading rumors about you, be the BIGGER person and forgive. Sooner or later, the truth will be revealed and those that talked about you will destroy their own character. One day, I was just working on some things with my business and all of a sudden God spoke to my spirit and said, "Pray for your enemies. Love your enemies" and started revealing their faces.

I was like, "Wow God, I did not even know they were secretly saying negative things about me". I did not question God and prayed for them like He said and I still love on them until this day as if I do not know. I received so much peace about everything!

CONFESSION:

I will choose what I talk about wisely and will not participate in gossiping, judging or spreading lies. The things I say can either help someone or could either cause someone to fall. Even the words I speak over myself from this day on will be positive. The words I speak today create my tomorrow and I have a great, wonderful life!

CHAPTER 4

1 + 1 = 2 or Does It?

ME, MYSELF, AND HIM:

Just because someone is single does not mean they are miserable. If you know of someone in a relationship, it does not mean they are happy.

YOU'RE VALUABLE:

Being single can be an enjoyable time where you discover who you are as a person. This is the time where you get to fully appreciate and enjoy your solo time. As a single woman, I love traveling the world, focusing on bettering myself as an individual and being positioned for what I was called to do in life. When God brings the man He wants me to be with that is compatible, I will be prepared so we can grow together spiritually, mentally, and financially. I will appreciate it much more because I know my worth now and already have things in place and going for myself.

My future husband will have things in place going for himself too. When marriage takes place, we both will be established and have individual things to bring to the table, while accomplishing our goals together.

So many times women want a man that is one of the following:

- Extremely attractive but with no ambition.

- Has lots and lots of money but has a tantrum when things do not go his way and your opinion does not matter.

- The smooth guy that you absolutely know is not going to work and does not want a commitment but you just love what he whispers, in your ear. The messed up part is you know for a fact he has at least three other women he is doing the same thing to!

FACT: You cannot change or trick a man into wanting to be with you. I repeat, you cannot change or trick a man into wanting to be with you! If that relationship is not approved by God, it may last or look good for a little bit but it will fail and do not be surprised when it does.

Stop giving your time to someone who wants you only for your vagina. When he finds it fit to not want to be bothered with you anymore because he is bored with you, he will move on to the next one. He will walk away just that quick, with your tears and all. Why do you keep giving your time to someone who only talks about your looks, your body and what he wants to do with you? Why do you keep dropping your pants to the ground just because he said the both of you will be together forever, after two weeks of meeting him? It is cool to save yourself for your husband! It will save you from heartache and unnecessary emotions.

Have you ever had your life planned out that by certain dates you were going to do this and by this age do that? I did that. By the age of 23 I was supposed to be married and have a business that was worldwide, by 24 have my first child, at 26 have my second child, and if I wanted another child have my third and last one by 29. My thinking back then was I did not want to be considered "old" and just now getting married and starting a family. I was thinking the right way wanting to be married and have children but it is all about timing, God's timing.

Now that I look back on my "life planning" from back then, I was not ready! I am glad I did not have those things happen then because I simply would not have been ready. I was truly not prepared to handle all of that during that time.

As I have matured, I will not date just because a man is fine, has lots of money or because everyone else is in a relationship. You should not base those things on why you feel you need to be in a relationship. When you date someone, it should be to see if he qualifies for the ultimate goal, which is marriage. It is cool to date and not have sex or not do sexual things until marriage. Treat your vagina like your social security number or debit card number. Do not give it out, protect it, and save it for your husband. If you do not protect or save it, it is going to keep getting used up by someone that is not worthy to have it in the first place! That is a piece of you that you can never get back once it is given up.

I sometimes hear from some men that they find me intimidating and upfront yet down to earth and gentle. One day, I asked, "What makes me intimidating"? The response was, "You know what you want out of life, doing what it takes to get there, and not willing to allow just anybody in your life". If knowing what I want out of life, taking the actions to get there, and being cautious about who I let into my life is considered "intimidating" to someone, well, I guess that is right! Even though I do not feel I am intimidating, I just know what I want and I am not about to let anyone distract me or waste my time.

Do not feel bad if someone comes to you with that stating you are intimidating because you have goals, ambition, a plan, enjoying your solo life, working on your purpose and waiting until marriage before anything sexual pops off. Guess what? God is going to send you a man that is compatible and does not feel intimidated, supports you and gets excited about your dream path! He is going to send someone that will respect you enough to honor your request to hold off from sex until marriage.

Keep your focus on God, school, work, and your purpose. When God sees you are busy and serious about His business and your purpose, He will send you the perfect man to add to it. Just be patient and do not be in a rush.

CONFESSION:

I will wait and keep myself until my king finds me and get married. My main focus is God, getting into my purpose, and school or work. Until then, I will remain happy and content with my singleness as I prepare to be a better person and a helpmate, for my future husband. I am truly worth the wait and I will not settle for less!

CHAPTER 5

I HAVE TO FIND MY PURPOSE

PURPOSE PROTECTOR:

Everyone has a purpose but it is up to you to find it, develop it and run with it. What is yours?

AND ACTION!:

You know you have been placed on this earth for a reason but is your issue finding out the reason? I have a lot of things I enjoy doing and even passionate about and I found out through all of them my purpose. For example, I love to mentor youth/young adults, write spoken word, travel and business. Guess what? God has positioned me to do all of them and I absolutely enjoy every single one! Your talents and gifts are a clue to your purpose. My Pastor did a sermon on locating your purpose through the wisdom of God.

He gave out the secrets on how to know your purpose and carry it out. I applied what he said to my life because I was tired of going around and around and around trying to do things my way and never going anywhere. In one day, God spoke to my spirit to write this book and the details to put in it, just for you! Yes, God cares for and loves you that much for you not to miss your destiny and for you to not have those thoughts about your life being worthless. He knows what you are going through and knows what you need to hear. He is not done with you yet so do not be done with yourself! He just wants your time so He can reveal your purpose through the gifts He has given you just the same way He has done for me. Yes, you are good enough!

CONFESSION:

I have a great life ahead of me! I will not waste my gifts or talents. I will use them to achieve my purpose. I know what I'm passionate about is a hint and an important part to getting there. I will not let anyone stop me or talk me out of my destiny. I will not quit along my journey and I will hold on to my hope.

YOU

Reading this book…..

Keep

Moving

FORWARD!

CHAPTER 6

FRIEND OR NOT

NO RESETS:

Friends are like cell phones. When you have all of your bars giving a strong signal they do not block you from reaching out connecting to your dreams. Friends can also be like having no bars. They block you from connecting to your goals, setting you back having you keep pushing redial and everything in your life always being re, re, re.

MAKE THE RIGHT DECISION:

Some of the people you are hanging with, you already know they are not supposed to be in your life like that. Since you all have been knowing each other forever, you don't see any harm being around them, right? WRONG!

When you have a vision of where you want to go and what you want to do in life, it is time to raise your right hand up, and wave from left to right to say bye-bye to some of those friends. Go ahead, practice waving right now. Keeping them is like piling up five people in a two-seater car. It is going to block your vision from moving forward, there's not enough room, you are going to get pulled over by the cops for everyone not being in a seatbelt being disobedient, and get a ticket that you will have to pay! Your friends are not even going to help you pay for the ticket either!!

Some will congratulate you, smile, jump up for joy, even may do a backbend for you but secretly inside, they do not really want you to be successful. They are not really happy for you because you know what you want in life and they are too scared to do those things. Have you ever dreamed so huge that people laughed at you like it was a joke and told you there is no way it can happen? Oh, but there is a way!!! Your dreams were meant for you only to understand. That's why it was given to you because you are just that bold to do it!!

Sometimes it is best to just keep it to yourself and not share while working on your plan.

Then, there are those true friends that are really, genuinely excited and happy for you. They know when they cheer you on they can be next and you will be right there to cheer them on as well. How do you know the fakes from the real? I'll tell you how! You will find out all about that in the last most important chapter, in this book!

CONFESSION:

I will choose my friends and the people I surround myself with wisely. If they do not motivate, encourage, are users, always speak negative towards me and my dreams, I will not hang around them. If they do not have the same outlook as I do about life, I will still love them but love them from a distance. This way I will not have to constantly push the replay button, in my life. I'm pushing play and continuing to move forward.

CHAPTER 7

JESUS MAKES IT ALL BETTER

ENOUGH SAID:

The title to this chapter does not need an introduction.

GOD REALLY DOES HAVE YOU:

All of the things were said in the previous chapters, to lead to this specific chapter, the most important one of all, a spiritual lifestyle. Someone may be asking, What does being spiritual have to do with my life, dreams, friends, family, mind, or heart? Everything!!! Or you might ask, "How do I have a spiritual lifestyle"? Having a personal relationship with God can turn everything around by the time you finish this sentence. How do you have a personal relationship with God?

First, getting saved (confess with your mouth and believe in your heart Jesus was raised from the dead and He still walks the earth today) and being filled with the Holy Spirit. Once this is done join a Christian, word of faith church. This is where the man/woman of God (Pastor) teaches the word of God (from the Bible), demonstrates how to apply the word from the Bible to your life daily, and he/she applies the word daily to his/her life, leading by example.

Invest in yourself and get a Bible. This will be one of the most valuable investments you will ever make, in your life. Read the Word and declare out loud what it says about you! The Bible has all of the answers to every question you may have now, in the future, and even in the past. Read the word daily, spend time with God through prayer and worship. The reason it is important to fellowship with other believers is because faith comes by hearing and hearing the word of God, so you won't give up! Do not listen to people who say you do not need to go to church, God knows your heart and that if you know His word you know God for yourself.

You not only want to know God, you also want God to know you. Just because someone can quote a scripture in the Bible does not guarantee a seat in Heaven. Satan knows the word and he is NEVER getting back in Heaven.

For the exact opposite, just because someone goes to church all of the time does not guarantee a seat in Heaven because if they have hate or unforgiveness in their heart, secretly hating, gossiping, being negative, then they missed it.

BUT, if someone has done bad things in the past, turns away from those things not doing them again, gets saved and filled with the Holy Spirit, read and do God's word, in the Bible, that makes God happy! He will start revealing to you what your purpose is, who to hang around, what things are good or bad for you and so much more! Yes, He will do it and keep on doing it as long as you put Him first. We spend 40 hours on a job, 8 hours in school, talking to people and getting to know them, learning about them, which is easy. So why is it so hard for us to take time out to give to God everyday, the One that can give us immediate answers?

He can give an answer to your problem in one second that can shift your entire life. I know for a fact He can because He did it for me! Quit listening to people that do not want anything out of life. Stop letting people live their life through you. You are held responsible for your life! Do not waste it because you only get one. What will happen if you go hard after your dreams? I know! You will reach them. Do not get discouraged and do not delay! Prepare that outstanding life of yours, not now, but RIGHT now!

CONCLUSION

Don't beat yourself up about the past. If you have done or doing any of these things discussed in this book, stop now and just move forward and do right. God does not focus on your past and neither should you. Just turn the other way. In order to get something different in your life, do different and accept change. Of course it may be uncomfortable or at times it may seem like you want to stop. You can't stop though because you are not a quitter! Just because you are not seeing immediate results does not require you to give up on everything that was planned for you. The only way you can reach your destiny is if you do not quit! That is it. Is your life worth fighting for to get your dreams from a thought into reality? Remember earlier you declared out loud, "I am worth it"! So, whatever is worth fighting for you have to keep on pressing, pushing, crawling, walking, and running until the thing you hoped for appears before your eyes. Love yourself and everything about you.

Love others and forgive quickly. Even if the other person is in the wrong and you know it, FORGIVE and forget it. Sometimes it may seem hard to be the bigger person but it is not up to you to handle it. Let God handle it. He is the One that fights your battles anyway so stop trying to fight them yourself.

SCRIPTURES

===============================

The following are some scriptures that were in or associated with the chapters, in this book. There are many scriptures you can read that relate to the following subjects. The following are quick references, taken from the New International Version (NIV) Bible, that can help you with overcoming a particular situation, receive encouragement or be inspired.

AFRAID:
Psalms 56:1-4
1 Be merciful to me, my God, for my enemies are in hot pursuit; all day long they press their attack. **2** My adversaries pursue me all day long; in their pride many are attacking me. **3** When I am afraid, I put my trust in you. **4** In God, whose word I praise—in God I trust and am not afraid. What can mere mortals do to me?

ALCOHOL:
Proverbs 20:1
1 Wine is a mocker and beer a brawler; whoever is led astray by them is not wise.

ANGER:
Ephesians 4:26-27
26 "In your anger do not sin"[d]: Do not let the sun go down while you are still angry, **27** and do not give the devil a foothold.

ANOTHER DAY:
Lamentations 3:22-23
22 Because of the Lord's great love we are not consumed, for his compassions never fail.**23** They are new every morning; great is your faithfulness.

BEAUTY:
1 Peter 3:3-4
3 Your beauty should not come from outward adornment, such as elaborate hairstyles and the wearing of gold jewelry or fine clothes. **4** Rather, it should be that of your inner self, the unfading beauty of a gentle and quiet spirit, which is of great worth in God's sight.

BELIEVE:
Matthew 21:22
22 If you believe, you will receive whatever you ask for in prayer."

BOLDNESS:
Ephesians 3:12
12 In him and through faith in him we may approach God with freedom and confidence.

BODY:
1 Corinthians 6:19-20
16 Do you not know that he who unites himself with a prostitute is one with her in body? For it is said, "The two will become one flesh."[b] **17** But whoever is united with the Lord is one with him in spirit.[c] **18** Flee from sexual immorality. All other sins a person commits are outside the body, but whoever sins sexually, sins against their own body. **19** Do you not know that your bodies are temples of the Holy Spirit, who is in you, whom you have received from God? You are not your own; **20** you were bought at a price. Therefore honor God with your bodies.

BULLYING:
Leviticus 19:18
18 "'Do not seek revenge or bear a grudge against anyone among your people, but love your neighbor as yourself. I am the Lord.

COMPETITION:
Philippians 2:3-4
3 Do nothing out of selfish ambition or vain conceit. Rather, in humility value others above yourselves, **4** not looking to your own interests but each of you to the interests of the others.

CONFUSION:
2 Corinthians 10:3-5
3 For though we live in the world, we do not wage war as the world does. **4** The weapons we fight with are not the weapons of the world. On the contrary, they have divine power to demolish strongholds. **5** We demolish arguments and every pretension that sets itself up against the knowledge of God, and we take captive every thought to make it obedient to Christ.

CURSING:
James 3:10
10 Out of the same mouth come praise and cursing. My brothers and sisters, this should not be.

DECEPTION:
James 1:22-25
22 Do not merely listen to the word, and so deceive yourselves. Do what it says. **23** Anyone who listens to the word but does not do what it says is like someone who looks at his face in a mirror **24** and, after looking at himself, goes away and immediately forgets what he looks like. **25** But whoever looks intently into the perfect law that gives freedom, and continues in it—not forgetting what they have heard, but doing it—they will be blessed in what they do.

DEFEAT:

Romans 8:38-39

38 For I am convinced that neither death nor life, neither angels nor demons,[k] neither the present nor the future, nor any powers, **39** neither height nor depth, nor anything else in all creation, will be able to separate us from the love of God that is in Christ Jesus our Lord.

DEPRESSION:

2 Corinthians 1:3-4

3 Praise be to the God and Father of our Lord Jesus Christ, the Father of compassion and the God of all comfort, **4** who comforts us in all our troubles, so that we can comfort those in any trouble with the comfort we ourselves receive from God.

DISCERNMENT:

1 John 4:1-3

1 Dear friends, do not believe every spirit, but test the spirits to see whether they are from God, because many false prophets have gone out into the world. **2** This is how you can recognize the Spirit of God: Every spirit that acknowledges that Jesus Christ has come in the flesh is from God, **3** but every spirit that does not acknowledge Jesus is not from God.

DOUBT:

Proverbs 3:5-6

5 Trust in the Lord with all your heart and lean not on your own understanding; **6** in all your ways submit to him, and he will make your paths straight.[a]

DRUGS:

2 Corinthians 7:1

1 Therefore, since we have these promises, dear friends, let us purify ourselves from everything that contaminates body and spirit, perfecting holiness out of reverence for God.

ENVY:

Proverbs 14:30

30 A heart at peace gives life to the body, but envy rots the bones.

EXCUSES:

Luke 14:17-24

17 At the time of the banquet he sent his servant to tell those who had been invited, 'Come, for everything is now ready.'

18 "But they all alike began to make excuses. The first said, 'I have just bought a field, and I must go and see it. Please excuse me.'

19 "Another said, 'I have just bought five yoke of oxen, and I'm on my way to try them out. Please excuse me.' **20** "Still another said, 'I just got married, so I can't come.'

21 "The servant came back and reported this to his master. Then the owner of the house became angry and ordered his servant, 'Go out quickly into the streets and alleys of the town and bring in the poor, the crippled, the blind and the lame.'

22 "'Sir,' the servant said, 'what you ordered has been done, but there is still room.' **23** "Then the master told his servant, 'Go out to the roads and country lanes and compel them to come in, so that my house will be full. **24** I tell you, not one of those who were invited will get a taste of my banquet.'"

FAITH:

Romans 10:17

17 Consequently, faith comes from hearing the message, and the message is heard through the word about Christ.

FEAR:

2 Timothy 1:7

7 For the Spirit God gave us does not make us timid, but gives us power, love and self-discipline.

FOCUS:
Proverbs 4:25
25 Let your eyes look straight ahead; fix your gaze directly before you.

FOGIVENESS:
Ephesians 4:31-32
31 Get rid of all bitterness, rage and anger, brawling and slander, along with every form of malice. **32** Be kind and compassionate to one another, forgiving each other, just as in Christ God forgave you.

FRIENDS:
Proverbs 12:26
26 The righteous choose their friends carefully, but the way of the wicked leads them astray.

GOSSIP:
2 Timothy 2:16-17
16 Avoid godless chatter, because those who indulge in it will become more and more ungodly. **17** Their teaching will spread like gangrene.

HATE:
1 John 4:20
20 Whoever claims to love God yet hates a brother or sister is a liar. For whoever does not love their brother and sister, whom they have seen, cannot love God, whom they have not seen.

HEALING:
1 Peter 2:24
24 "He himself bore our sins" in his body on the cross, so that we might die to sins and live for righteousness; "by his wounds you have been healed."

HEAR GOD'S VOICE:
Jeremiah 33:3
3 'Call to me and I will answer you and tell you great and unsearchable things you do not know.'

HEART:
Proverbs 4:23
23 Above all else, guard your heart, for everything you do flows from it.

HEARTACHE:
Psalm 34:17-20
17 The righteous cry out, and the Lord hears them; he delivers them from all their troubles.18 The Lord is close to the brokenhearted and saves those who are crushed in spirit. 19 The righteous person may have many troubles, but the Lord delivers him from them all; 20 he protects all his bones, not one of them will be broken.

HEARTBREAK:
Psalms 147:3
3 He heals the brokenhearted and binds up their wounds.

HONESTY:
Luke 16:10
10 "Whoever can be trusted with very little can also be trusted with much, and whoever is dishonest with very little will also be dishonest with much.

HOPE:
Hebrews 11:1
11 Now faith is confidence in what we hope for and assurance about what we do not see.

HUMBLE:
1 Peter 5:6
6 Humble yourselves, therefore, under God's mighty hand, that he may lift you up in due time.

HURT:
Exodus 14:14
14 The Lord will fight for you; you need only to be still."

IDOL:
Leviticus 26:1
1 "'Do not make idols or set up an image or a sacred stone for yourselves, and do not place a carved stone in your land to bow down before it. I am the Lord your God.

INCREASE:
Ephesians 3:20
20 Now to him who is able to do immeasurably more than all we ask or imagine, according to his power that is at work within us,

IMPURE THOUGHT:
1 Corinthians 10:13
13 No temptation[c] has overtaken you except what is common to mankind. And God is faithful; he will not let you be tempted[d] beyond what you can bear. But when you are tempted,[e] he will also provide a way out so that you can endure it.

JEALOUS:
Galatians 5:14-15
14 For the entire law is fulfilled in keeping this one command: "Love your neighbor as yourself."[b] 15 If you bite and devour each other, watch out or you will be destroyed by each other.

JOY:
James 1:2-3
2 Consider it pure joy, my brothers and sisters,[a] whenever you face trials of many kinds, 3 because you know that the testing of your faith produces perseverance.

LEADER:
Proverbs 11:14
14 For lack of guidance a nation falls, but victory is won through many advisers.

LOVE:
1 Corinthians 13:4-8
4 Love is patient, love is kind. It does not envy, it does not boast, it is not proud. **5** It does not dishonor others, it is not self-seeking, it is not easily angered, it keeps no record of wrongs. **6** Love does not delight in evil but rejoices with the truth. **7** It always protects, always trusts, always hopes, always perseveres. **8** Love never fails.

LUST:
1 Corinthians 6:18
18 Flee from sexual immorality. All other sins a person commits are outside the body, but whoever sins sexually, sins against their own body.

LYING:
Proverbs 12:22
22 The Lord detests lying lips, but he delights in people who are trustworthy.

MANIPULATION:
Matthew 24:4
4 Jesus answered: "Watch out that no one deceives you.

MIND:
Romans 12:2
2 Do not conform to the pattern of this world, but be transformed by the renewing of your mind. Then you will be able to test and approve what God's will is—his good, pleasing and perfect will.

NATURAL:
1 Corinthians 2:14
4 The person without the Spirit does not accept the things that come from the Spirit of God but considers them foolishness, and cannot understand them because they are discerned only through the Spirit.

PATIENCE:

Hebrews 10:36

36 You need to persevere so that when you have done the will of God, you will receive what he has promised.

PEACE:

John 14:27

7 Peace I leave with you; my peace I give you. I do not give to you as the world gives. Do not let your hearts be troubled and do not be afraid.

PRAISE:

Daniel 2:23

23 I thank and praise you, God of my ancestors: You have given me wisdom and power, you have made known to me what we asked of you, you have made known to us the dream of the king."

PRAYER:

Philippians 4:6

6 Do not be anxious about anything, but in every situation, by prayer and petition, with thanksgiving, present your requests to God.

PRESSURE:

Proverbs 3:25-26

25 Have no fear of sudden disaster or of the ruin that overtakes the wicked, **26** for the Lord will be at your side and will keep your foot from being snared.

PRIDE:

Proverbs 16:18

18 Pride goes before destruction, a haughty spirit before a fall.

PROSPERITY:

Deuteronomy 8:18

18 But remember the Lord your God, for it is he who gives you the ability to produce wealth, and so confirms his covenant, which he swore to your ancestors, as it is today.

PURPOSE:

Jeremiah 1:5

5 "Before I formed you in the womb I knew[a] you, before you were born I set you apart; I appointed you as a prophet to the nations."

PURITY:

Psalm 119:9

9 How can a young person stay on the path of purity? By living according to your word.

REBELLION:

1 Peter 3:10

10 For, "Whoever would love life and see good days must keep their tongue from evil and their lips from deceitful speech.

REJECTION:

Deuteronomy 14:2

2 for you are a people holy to the Lord your God. Out of all the peoples on the face of the earth, the Lord has chosen you to be his treasured possession.

RELATIONSHIPS:

Matthew 22:37-39

37 Jesus replied: "'Love the Lord your God with all your heart and with all your soul and with all your mind.'[c] **38** This is the first and greatest commandment. **39** And the second is like it: 'Love your neighbor as yourself.'[d]

REVENGE:
Proverbs 14:16-17
16 The wise fear the Lord and shun evil, but a fool is hotheaded and yet feels secure. **17** A quick-tempered person does foolish things, and the one who devises evil schemes is hated.

REWARD:
Galatians 6:9
9 Let us not become weary in doing good, for at the proper time we will reap a harvest if we do not give up.

SAVED:
Romans 10:9-10
9 If you declare with your mouth, "Jesus is Lord," and believe in your heart that God raised him from the dead, you will be saved. **10** For it is with your heart that you believe and are justified, and it is with your mouth that you profess your faith and are saved.

SEX:
1 Thessalonians 4:3-6
3 It is God's will that you should be sanctified: that you should avoid sexual immorality; **4** that each of you should learn to control your own body[a] in a way that is holy and honorable, **5** not in passionate lust like the pagans, who do not know God; **6** and that in this matter no one should wrong or take advantage of a brother or sister.[b]

SICKNESS:
Jeremiah 30:17
17 But I will restore you to health and heal your wounds,' declares the Lord, 'because you are called an outcast, Zion for whom no one cares.'

SIN:
Proverbs 5:22-23
22 The evil deeds of the wicked ensnare them; the cords of their sins hold them fast. **23** For lack of discipline they will die, led astray by their own great folly.

SPIRITUAL:
Ephesians 3:16-19
16 I pray that out of his glorious riches he may strengthen you with power through his Spirit in your inner being, **17** so that Christ may dwell in your hearts through faith. And I pray that you, being rooted and established in love, **18** may have power, together with all the Lord's holy people, to grasp how wide and long and high and deep is the love of Christ, **19** and to know this love that surpasses knowledge—that you may be filled to the measure of all the fullness of God.

STEALING:
Ephesians 4:28
28 Anyone who has been stealing must steal no longer, but must work, doing something useful with their own hands, that they may have something to share with those in need.

STRENGTH:
1 Chronicles 16:11
11 Look to the Lord and his strength; seek his face always.

SUICIDE:
1 Corinthians 3:16-17
6 Don't you know that you yourselves are God's temple and that God's Spirit dwells in your midst? **17** If anyone destroys God's temple, God will destroy that person; for God's temple is sacred, and you together are that temple.

SWEARING:
Colossians 3:8
8 But now you must also rid yourselves of all such things as these: anger, rage, malice, slander, and filthy language from your lips.

TONGUE:
Proverbs 18:21
21 The tongue has the power of life and death, and those who love it will eat its fruit.

TRUST:
Proverbs 3:5-6
5 Trust in the Lord with all your heart and lean not on your own understanding; **6** in all your ways submit to him, and he will make your paths straight.[a]

UNBELIEF:
Hebrews 3:12-13
12 See to it, brothers and sisters, that none of you has a sinful, unbelieving heart that turns away from the living God. **13** But encourage one another daily, as long as it is called "Today," so that none of you may be hardened by sin's deceitfulness.

UNFORGIVENESS:
Matthew 18:21-22
21 Then Peter came to Jesus and asked, "Lord, how many times shall I forgive my brother or sister who sins against me? Up to seven times?" **22** Jesus answered, "I tell you, not seven times, but seventy-seven times.[g]

UNIQUE:
Psalms 139:14
14 I praise you because I am fearfully and wonderfully made; your works are wonderful, I know that full well.

WIN:
Philippians 4:13
13 I can do all this through him who gives me strength.

WISDOM:

Proverbs 9:10

10 The fear of the Lord is the beginning of wisdom, and knowledge of the Holy One is understanding.

WORK:

Colossians 3:23

23 Whatever you do, work at it with all your heart, as working for the Lord, not for human masters,

WORRY:

Isaiah 35:3-4

3 Strengthen the feeble hands, steady the knees that give way; **4** say to those with fearful hearts, "Be strong, do not fear; your God will come, he will come with vengeance; with divine retribution he will come to save you."

WORSHIP:

John 4:23-24

23 Yet a time is coming and has now come when the true worshipers will worship the Father in the Spirit and in truth, for they are the kind of worshipers the Father seeks. **24** God is spirit, and his worshipers must worship in the Spirit and in truth."

POEM JUST FOR YOU

Out of the many people in the world, I refuse to stay the same.
An average life is not for me, I'm ready for change.

For change to come, it starts with me, believing in me.
Like the eagles that spread their wings to soar, I'm accountable
for my destiny.

A winner, conqueror, and a leader, yes I win.
Making the right choices and surrounding myself with positive
people, through good associations.

Beauty, intelligence, talents and gifts shining from inside, out.
Selecting my words carefully, I have what I say eliminating
all doubt.

It was promised to me when I do my part, as long as I don't quit,
I'm guaranteed to succeed.
I'm for team Jesus and everything God said about His fearfully and
wonderfully made creation, me, I believe I have it, so therefore I
receive.

- Devon Chestnut

CONTACT INFORMATION

Email: devchestnut@gmail.com

Phone: (786) 507.8204

FB Page: www.facebook.com/ladies4apurpose

(Like and Comment on the FB Page)

Made in the USA
Lexington, KY
14 July 2018